HARBIN(

EDITOR-IN-CHIEF: Dustin Pickering
ASSISTANT EDITOR: Z. M. Wise

Contact Dustin Pickering for submissions:
desireofdogs@gmail.com

HARBINGER ASYLUM is an quarterly literary magazine.

Printed in the United States of America by:
CreateSpace

ISBN-13:
978-1493615780

ISBN-10:
1493615785

Look for us at: *www.harbingerasylum.wordpress.com*

HARBINGER ASYLUM is published by
TRANSCENDENT ZERO PRESS

You never know what you will find inside...

HARBINGER ASYLUM!

This issue reins in a new feature thanks to a suggestion by one of our poets, PW Covington. We decided to include book reviews from independent authors along with the usual political column and its wild perspective.

We also bring you, our reader, a slice of Nina Nicole's short fiction called *Dangerous Love*. It is a vampire tale and it will provoke excitement, lust, and fear of carnage.

Recently I traveled to Edinburg, Texas for the Beat Fest organized by Christopher Carmona. Edinburg is located near the Tex-Mex border where Billy Burroughs grew up. We had an anthology reading, many featured performances, and a good party after the entire event was coming to a close. PW jumped in the hotel bar's fountain, and we were drunk as we ran to the golf course for a rattlesnake séance. To make it short, Burroughs is rumored to have killed a rattlesnake at that location. We stayed at the Echo Hotel and they hosted our featured readings. All in all, I met some wonderful people including (but not limited to) Opalina Salas, Edward Vidaurre, and Erika Garza-Johnson with her husband, Rob. Everyone had great stories to tell and I came home with a knapsack of them myself.

Yes, friends and colleagues, poetry is alive and making its way across the globe. This includes *Harbinger Asylum,* so if you have words to share with the literary type send them to me, the Editor-in-Chief. My email is located in the frontpiece of this publication.

This issue is packed gloriously with beautiful poetry and has a cover painted by Chad Sorg. You can find his musings and/or visual art online. He even sells many of his remarkable works.

As the holidays approach, we are preparing a wonderful anthology for gifts to poets and peers. It will be called *To Hold A Moment Still*. We are continuing to build Transcendent Zero Press, and have two books already published by respected authors. One is *Passion's Zest* by Marcie Eanes, and the other is a collection by Ken Jones called *Mr. Karma*. Feel free to support our growing press by having a look on Amazon.com for these poetry sensations. I am myself preparing my first full length book for release. I have begun one called *The Future of Poetry is Now: Bones Picking at Death's Howl*, but my first collection is titled *The Daunting Ephemeral*.

As for bad news, the Coffee Oasis First Monday Reading Series is completely canceled because of recent changes in ownership. I have heard a variety of rumors but the only thing I can say for certain is I have called the store and spoken with the manager. All I was told is, "Currently, this doesn't seem to be the venue for that. If anything changes, I'll call you." That is the owner Sharms' way of asking me to find another venue for our reading series. This is the way I am repaid for hosting the series, and the lack of professionalism from Sharms a week before the big Texas Poetry Calendar reading is unacceptable. This final reading of the year brings the editors of Dos Gatos Press from Austin, Texas to host featured performers who are published in the calendar. Rumor has it the store is being steered toward becoming a wine bar and bistro under Sharms' ownership. Neither Sharms nor Rusty, the former owner, are permitted to speak against each other while the case is being handled in court. It does look like we have lost a piece of the art community where not only poets could share their work, but also aspiring young musicians and talented painters would showcase their gifts. This is the way the world ends…not with a bang, but a whimper.

Thank you one and all for supporting *Harbinger Asylum*.

Editor-in-Chief, *Dustin D. Pickering*

CONTENTS

Biographies / 7-10

Ode to a Corduroy Coat by PW Covington / 11-12

Calli of the Three Moons by Terry Jude Miller/ 13

The Working Man by Terry Jude Miller / 14-15

Weary Street Revolver by Z.M. Wise / 15

Counting Flamingoes by Terry Jude Miller / 16

Faith Running Away From Me by Z.M. Wise/ 17

Split Faces with Faces by Z.M. Wise / 18

Josephine wishes her name was psychopompus by Stephen Defferari / 19-20

Just Arrived by Ellen Reich / 21-22

If I Had Been A Flyboy in WWII by Ellen Reich / 22

Bissonnet Boulevard Dogs by Winston Derden / 23

The Horde's Prayer by Winston Derden / 24

Mother's Eyes by Nicholas Bailey / 25-26

Origin by Linda Bratcher Wlodyka/ 27

Dance Underwater by Birdman 313 / 28

Your Last Friend by Birdman 313 / 29-30

Victory by Chuck Taylor / 30-31

I pour a shot of whisky (for Barry) by Chicory Poetry / 31

The Prose Poem and Einstein by Chuck Taylor/ 32-33

Prose Poem Speaks by Chuck Taylor / 33

Dangerous Love (excerpts) by Nina Nicole / 34-35

This Light by Dustin Pickering / 36

Unaware by Dustin Pickering / 36

How Far by Dustin Pickering/ 37

Incarnate Choice by Dustin Pickering / 38

An Early Poem Concerning Catholicism by Dustin Pickering/ 38

Synapses by Leisl Weaver Miller/ 39

Paper Doll by Leisl Weaver Miller / 40-41

Caretaker Mingles by Chad Sorg/ 42

Human Pains and Growing Stains by John Davidson / 43

Judas by Proximity by John Davidson / 44

The Book of Life by Chicory Poetry / 45

My Country, Too by Marcie Eanes / 46

Texas Vision Center by Richard Peake / 47

Occupation by Jenuine Poetess / 48-50

Wind Song by Carmen Jacobsen / 50

Hushed by Patricia Oliman Longoria / 51

Waterplay at the Base of Luther's Canyon by David Cowen/ 52

BOOK REVIEWS:
"I Took My Barrio on a Road Trip" *(Edward Viduarre)*
by PW Covington / 53
"Earth and Stars" (Richard Peake)
by Dustin Pickering / 54
NOT QUITE A POLITICAL COLUMN / 55

BIOGRAPHIES

Dustin Pickering is a featured poet at Public Poetry 2013, and hosts two separate readings in the Houston area. He is published in the Muse for Women anthology, *The Beatest State in the Union, Blind Vigil Revue*, and many other anthologies and smaller publications. He is our Editor-in-Chief.

Terry Jude Miller is a published and award winning poet from Houston, Texas. The recipient of the 2012 Mildred Vorpahl Baass & Nancy Baass Poetry Award, a Juried Poet for the 2011 & 2012 Houston Poetry Festival and winner of the Global Peace Poem competition of the 2012 Tyler Peace Festival, his work has been published in scores of publications including Everyday Poets, the University of Houston's Bayou Review, Ancient Paths, Orbis, Stepping Stones Magazine, Furnace Review, Shine Journal, Blue Skies Poetry, Survivor's Review, Live Oak Review, Lamplighter Review, Bijou Poetry Review, Chaffey Review, Foundling Review, Houston Literary Review, Boston Literary Magazine, and the Edison Literary Review. In January 2010, his poem, "The Diagnosis", appeared in the Birmingham Arts Journal. He has read his poetry at venues in the UK and the United States. Miller's books of poetry, are titled: "The Day I Killed Superman", "What If I Find Only Moonlight?", and "The Butterfly Canonical" and can be purchased at barnesandnoble.com, booksamillion.com, amazon.com,itunes.com, lulu.com and other book vendor sites. He is a member of the Academy of American Poets, the Poetry Society of Texas, the Gulf Coast Poets Society, Poets Northwest (Houston), the founder of the Fort Bend Poets Group and the Fort Bend County Poet Laureate Competition. Terry is a retired professor of eMarketing and held an Innovation Fellowship at Kaplan University.

Stephen Defferari is 30, goes to UHCL, English-History major, lives in Clear Lake, originally from California, moved back here (family reasons), he writes poetry and plays.

Ellen Reich teaches creative writing for the Emeritus division of Santa Monica College. Her poems have been published in Los Angeles Times, Slant, Slipstream, ACM, Coe Review and others. She has won awards from DA Center for Arts, Blue Unicorn, Cape Cod Times etc. A chapbook, Reverse Kiss, was editor's choice and published by Main Street Rag in 2005. Her book, The Gynecic Papers, deals primary with women's issues. A recent chapbook was published by Finishing Line Press, entitled Sleeping Guardian. Her next poetry book is forthcoming from Tebot Bach, entitled Sacrifices Have To Be Human.

Winston Derden is a lapsed academic, apostate journalist, poet and fiction writer who resides in Houston. His short story "Rubato" appears in Able To... edited by Neil Ellis Orts. His poetry appears in New Texas, the 2011 Texas Poetry Calendar, and the Houston Poetry Festival Anthology for 2010. He is currently at work on his second novel.

Nicholas Bailey is a former student at San Jac college who now works 2 jobs. After realizing he could no longer pursue his dreams of paint and sculpture, he turned to poetry to express his imagination. Using concepts of love and paganism, he seeks to entertain readers with truths in life.

Linda Bratcher Wlodyka is a resident of Cheshire, in Western Massachusetts and works as an English/Literature/Writing, high school tutor in Williamstown. Her poems have been published in several journals: *Silkworm, Equinox, Poet's of Blood II, Avocet, Journal of Modern Poetry #15.* Linda has published 3 chapbooks titled, *My Spirited Cameo 2008, Voices from the Blue Room 2009* and *Tick Tock 2011.* Linda enjoys the company of teenagers, kayaking, floral arranging, and word games.

Birdman 313 has been writing Poetry since 1978–79 but been writing since I was 8 years old. I have 3 Poetry Books and 2 Poetry Chap Books published "Thoughts from the Mind", "Birdman13 Point1", and "Thoughts of Life (360 E. May St. B.H,. Mich) 2 Poetry Chap Books "Poems of Life", and "Poems of Dreams" with a 4th Poetry book to be released in 2014 and a Poetry chapbook sometime this year. Have been published in several poetry magazines and host the Spoken Word Contest at the National Black Book Festival.

Chuck Taylor has published two recent books of poetry, Heterosexual: A Love Song, and Li Po Laughing At the Lonely Moon. His most recent book is a memoir by Ink Brush Press called Saving Sebastian. It details a father's struggle with his son's drug abuse and addiction. He is also author of *The One True Cat.*

Chicory Poetry grew up in the isolated coal mining mountains of Virginia and began writing poetry and short stories at the age of nine. Previous publishing venues include: Casa Italian, The Connection, Unity Magazine, as well as the premier edition of Fragrance. Remembrance - whether real or imagined - is a reoccurring theme in his poetry.

Nina Nicole does not have a bio available. She is still working on *Dangerous Love* and has no set date for release.

Leisl Weaver Miller is a Friday's child that was born in the Year of the Fire Horse. Her childhood was spent living in many different areas of the North Eastern, Southern and the Mid-Western parts of the U. S. She studied Interior Design, Art History and Poetry in college. Leisl lists motherhood as her biggest accomplishment, but overcoming eating animals and smoking cigarettes do not trail much behind. She is challenged by all spiders and other creepy crawly creatures. She is proud of her dry sense of humor, her love for a God, and her sterling heart collection. She is always writing or thinking about writing which is why she is sleep deprived. She doesn't think much of sports or adult style cartoons, but living in a house where she is the only female makes it impossible to escape. Leisl is best known for her big heart; she is obsessed with rescuing animals and people alike.

Chad Sorg is an artist/author originally from Indiana. He was a co-disorganizer of the anarchist art-in-motels-event, NadaDada, featured in the New York Times. Sorg was once Goldfield's Chamber of Commerce president and chief artist at the International Car Forest of the Last Church. In his spare time he designs magazine covers and burns buses. Here's his blog: *www.fishbowler.wordpress.com*

John Davidson is a husband and father of three; he is also a writer of many things including poetry.

Marcie Eanes is an independent journalist and poet. Her writings have appeared in *Essence* and *Seventeen* magazines, and her poetry has been in numerous anthologies including *di-verse-city* 2011-13 and *Anthology of the Muse for Women: No to Violence Against Women*. Her first book, *Sensual Sounds,* explored all forms of loving relationships. With her latest book, *Passion's Zest,* she hopes to inspire others to live passionately and never take life for granted. At the age of 23, she experienced a life-threatening accident after which she reinvented her writing career. Today, she travels widely to promote her poetry. She has been published in *Harbinger Asylum* and *SpokenVizions Magazine,* the winner of National Poetry Awards "best magazine of the year" category in 2013. She currently resides in Racine, Wisconsin. She can be reached at *marcie_eanes2@yahoo.com.*

Richard Peake is a native Virginian who became a Texas resident after retiring from the University of Virginia's College at Wise. He published early poems in *Impetus* alongside John Ciardi and in the *Georgia Review.* Collections of his poetry are *Wings Across...* and *Poems for Terence* published by Vision Press. Recent poems have appeared in *Avocet, Asinine Poetry, Boundless 2010* and *2011, Nature Croons, Raven Images, Skive, Sol Magazine,* and *Shine Journal* (one nominated for a Pushcart Prize), and also in *Texas Poetry Calendar 2012* and *The Road Not Taken.* He is a father and grandfather, he teaches at the Osher Lifelong Learning Institute.

Jenuine Poetess is a poet, visionary, community organizer, and aunt currently based in Waco, Texas. She is the founder of In the Words of Womyn and is deeply delighted to witness the birth and thriving of two chapters of the writing circle in Sylmar, California and Waco, Texas. In January 2013, Jenuine founded The Word Gallery, a collection of programs—including a weekly open mic venue—which provide outlets for creative expression, with special focus on written and spoken-word arts. Jenuine was recently named Chair of the Waco Cultural Arts annual WordFest after her participation in the 2013 festival as coordinator, facilitator, and host of various workshops, readings, and open mics throughout the weekend. In addition to practicing her own writing craft, Jenuine is passionate about empowering herself and others to continually give sound to our story and volume to our voice.

PW Covington is a Texas poet that works as a PTSD recovery facilitator in rural and small communities with under-served Veterans and their family members. Additional biographical and bibliographical details about him and his work can be found here:
http://www.pwcovington.com/

Carmen Jacobsen is a non-fiction and poetry writer. She has written education articles for The Rice Entrepreneurship Educational Program Blog also known as REEP besides being a featured guest poet at the Barnes & Noble Poetry Series. Carmen has completed her first book of poems *Saudade* and is currently working on her second book, a collection of haikus inspired by her years of living in Cordova, AK. She loves to teach children how to sing, dance and write. She has set up musical plays for a Montessori school at the Bayou Theater at UH Clear Lake and directed a small *Ballet Folklorico* group named *Aztlan*, where children combined poetry with the Mexican *zapateado*. She has been a creative writing teacher for WITS – Writers in the Schools for eight years now.

Patricia Oliman Longoria is a 25 year member of The Poetry Roundtable, a 13 year member and Secretary of The Write Thoughts writing group, and a three year member of The Fellowship of Scribes. Present Administrator of the poetry and creative writing group Poetry and Stuff of Galveston, Texas. She began writing in 1979 and has come to discover that her work may not always be a work of art, but it is always a work of heart.

David Cowen is a trial attorney by trade. He has published a book of poems called *Sixth and Adams* (2001) and has been published online by George Mason University, Stephen F. Austin University, Sam Houston State University, and many other privately published journals. His poetry was featured in the Canadian Broadcasting Company's radio journal "Outfront" in a 2005 tribute on 9/11. His essay "On Motherhood" is published in a collection by Thisibelieve.org.

Z.M. Wise is a poet who has been writing before his first steps as a child. He aspires to spread the word (well, his words, to be exact) around the world. He has been published in numerous national and international anthologies and magazines. Z. M. says about poetry, "Do not hold your words captive as you would a feeble insect in a jar. Let them breathe and extend their eager hands to every pair of eyes and ears that crave an innovative touch of life." His first full length book *Take Me Back, Kingswood Clock!* is available from Amazon.com. Feel free to check out his About.me page. It includes a bio and links to his Facebook and YouTube pages.

http://about.me/ZMWisethePoet

Ode to a Corduroy Coat

PW Covington

I don't remember, for sure,
Just where I got this coat
This brown sport coat
This corduroy jacket
But, it might have been a South Austin thrift store in mid-Spring

It's a little ratty, a little worn
But the sleeves are long enough
And it's not too warm
This corduroy jacket;
Together, we've committed countless acts of poetry
From McAllen to Salt Lake City

This corduroy jacket is street-wise;
It's seen the French Quarter

I left it behind once
After a night of 3-way, power-exchange, sex
In a hotel room not far from the airport in San Antonio
But, it came back to me, the following week
Like something real and lasting
After the scent and sting of lust had gone

This corduroy jacket does not have suede patches on the sleeves
This corduroy jacket is a college drop-out
And, it is used to staying crumpled, behind a car seat, for months at a time
This corduroy jacket is my poetry - it fits me

It's got strange, hidden, inside pockets
It is out of place in Texas

I have other coats, but I wear it most
A favorite, sacred shield,
I wear it like safety gear
The full armor of my appetites
This corduroy jacket
Fits me, follows me, finds me
My wayward haberdashery
This corduroy jacket still has poems to tell and nights to welcome home.

Calli Of The Three Moons

Terry Jude Miller

In an endless night of keening,
the stars paste to the purple sky,
vibration-less in their vigil of sorrow.

No venal magistrate with whom to barter,
the solitary price to pay for this turning
is the heart's blood, the soul's last kindle.

Calli of the three moons,
brilliant in your slumber,
make room for the returning,
when love's orbit brings you 'round
atop the crown of an aurora borealis,
the edge of an angel's halo.

Loaves of challah will be stacked,
cups will overflow with celebration,
and the long path to heaven
will be forgotten,
released from your mother's bosom
like a great sigh of contentment.

The Working Man

Terry Jude Miller

like the tug of a dog
at his own tail,
my father's hand falls
from the arm of his chair,
his eyes closed, mouth open
in a hymn of silent glory

the heart beats in recall
resets the sun against
the farmer sky, there
are footsteps deep and confident
in the plowed earth
where more than seeds fall

it is not the enough
that silences the hungry heart,
it is the undiscovered beyond
the hill, where the sun rolls
itself into wonder

how many barns have I filled
and emptied in your example

how many fields have I
folded into fountains,
my blood running out

the turning has become
the reason for the wheel

in all the revolutions
I have not found
the peak, I see only
new mountain trees in the distance
that have not tasted my ax

littered along the way,
the thousand cries
for returning, but I am
too deep into the fields
to hear nor heed that pleading

Weary Street Revolver

Z.M. Wise

Loaded and armed to the teeth,
action is his middle name.
Dark alleyways, his sanctuary.

Rifle: no harm done.
Pistol: what a clear shot.
Misses his enemy like he misses his mother.

Bullets in his heart
that fill the holes of emptiness,
loneliness and lack of love.

No woman to caress;
just a naked gun as his bedfellow.
No action...just a metal contraption.

Too early to ponder,
too late to wander...
For the weary street revolver.

Counting Flamingos

Terry Jude Miller

Carolina scratches
a mark for each regal
flamingo head she counts

she stops as a single
downy-plumed chick
approaches

no anger, no fear,
only beauty, only grace

she cradles the bird's
white head
in her trembling palm

shaken by the act
of innocence, a tear
blooms on Carolina's
tan, star-freckled cheek

the bird gently presses
his shoehorn beak
against her breast

then pleads in avian-speak
to be included
with special remembrance
in Carolina's common-place ledger

Faith Running Away From Me

Z.M. Wise

Meager beams of the light source,
assume this blackened temple.
As I pray, always miserable, always blue.
Frozen here, waiting.

Hooded white forms molded in shards of glass
hover as dust bounces around in the air
shaping an image in my skull,
penetrating my blackened skin.

Boneless on a ghastly face,
I stand up,
now deferring
to this apocalyptic purgatory.

Split Faces with Faces

Z.M. Wise

Ancient mystic energy
bonds with the Star Children.

Cars will come and go,
but dashing princes will always ride the white horse.

Now, cross the eyes of boredom
as you stare at the gatekeeper named Ben.

Bottom of the psycho pit,
most serial killers feel absolutely no remorse.

Travel down to Hell's wishing well
and hear the pleading cries of the damned.

Wish away the evil; no effect at all.
Praise to the women who carefully sew.

Beware the messages from government insanity,
telling us that the very things we read are banned.

Split faces with faces, dear child,
and away we go!

Josephine wishes her name was psychopompus

Stephen Defferari

Man dies facedown at neighborhood park,
Kite he was flying still attached to clenched fist,
Loiters defiantly in the air afterwards like a
Kind of spiritual periscope, crashes into adjacent
Swing-set where truants talk about the
Advantages of megalomania, one picks up kite,
Jokes about the idyllic absurdity of kites in general,
Sees dead guy face down in grass rigidly postured
The way people stand in corners when punished,
Walks over to him, nudges with foot, stares
In blank apprehension, don't know what to do,
Thinks he is dead, says he thinks he is dead with
Dramatic emphasis between 'is' and 'dead',
Others agree, wonder why or how he died, suggest
That maybe he hung himself from a cloud,
Others say that isn't funny, takes out dead guy's
Wallet from suit pocket, find a lot of cash inside,
Think they should find someone older who will
Buy them beer and cigarettes, walk to a nearby
Gas-station, forget about finding someone else
Much older to tell about the body in the park with
The kite attached, young guy in leather jacket
Named Brandon pulls-up in old primer grey
Camaro listening to some sub-genre of metal, kids
Ask if he will be cool and buy them cigarettes
And beer and keep rest of cash for a tip, Brandon
Says ok, goes inside, buys some beer and smokes,
Goes back to car, gets in, kids look from around
The corner, distraught, vexed-teenager faces, shout
Something about being cool, Brandon tells them to
Fuck-off or he will kick their ass, peels out as he
Drives away, laughs to himself about how dumb
Kids are, opens smokes, lights, takes long, deep
Drags, nods head to the rhythm of the music,
Rests hand in between his legs, feels cool, looks

At sunset, shade and light form a horizontal line
That bisects his pupils perfectly, he thinks of
California, he thinks of beautiful yet empty ewers
For no reason, mumbles at old man in truck driving
Too close to his bumper, takes several short drags,
Turns up music involuntarily, slicks back hair, feels
Like he looks like Matt Dillon in that movie about
Avant-garde junkies, can't remember the name,
Doesn't matter, thinks about a girl named Josephine
Who wishes her name was psychopompos,
Her parents have a summer house in Acapulco, she
Smokes joints rolled in Bible paper under a bridge,
Lost virginity to Todd, worships pagan deities in a
Circle of candles in her mother's green house when
Everyone is asleep, Brandon calls Josephine, no
Answer, sun goes down, he drives over to her house,
Parks a few houses down, dad doesn't like him
Coming around, thinks he does drugs and uses a
Ouija board to Communicate with Elvis for style
Pointers, goes through back door by fence, throws
Pebbles at the window, she opens, holds finger over
Shut lips, she dresses, sneaks out room and down
Hall, mother crying in the other room with door
Ajar, tiptoes downstairs, goes out back door, they
Hug, walk to Camaro, get in, peels-out down street,
She lights joint and they talk, says something
About her mom being upset about dad, that he's
Flying away with a phenomenologist, Brandon
Doesn't know what that is, Josephine thinks its
Like an anesthesiologist, but with an exhilarative,
Rather than a sedative intent, drive to park,
Ambulance going the opposite way, park, get beer,
Walk over to the swing sets, sit, drink and smoke in
The dark, talk about the advantages of a dystopian
Society, Brandon sees kits limp in the grass, picks it
Up while tuning-out Josephine's stoned disquisition,
Flips it over, sees writing on the yellow nylon,
Spells 'Phenomenologist'.

Just Arrived

Ellen Reich

Crossing the country from New Jersey.
Hitting LA smog and concrete,
curving through the McClure tunnel, wondering.
Then I know.
The Pacific. Wild.
Damaging, demanding, damning undercurrent.
Waves soaring beyond abstraction.
My first Santa Ana.
Cool foggy evening transformed.
Blasts of desert heat blister my body, crack my lips.
Nose bleeds.
Folding chairs slide across the backyard deck.
Bang into railings.
Moon's snagged in the palm.
Fronds flung across the road.
A sky without cirrus clouds.
No rain upon no rain.
Then torrents unearth coffins.
Newness is brittle.
Wreathed seaweed beaches like dead whales.
Pelicans slide above the sea's crust, mute as stone.
Avocados soften.
Chili peppers bite my tongue.
More. I want more.
More eccentric food.
Hot sauce. Soft corn tortillas.
I feel like an immigrant
parachuted from a paper plane,
injured, inexact.
This is an occupied place.
I want to be seized.
Formed new.
Fire. Mountains draped in orange.
Chips, sweats, bottled water stuffed in sacks.
No time for photo albums, my father's letters.

I run to the beach.
Watch the red sun set on charred homes.
Feel seawater seep between my toes.
Lie down on a bed of coarse sand.
Dig my body in.

If I Had Been A Flyboy in WWII
Ellen Reich

I would have been captured on Chichi Jima
I would have resisted decoding American messages
I would have been tied to a tree
I would have been kicked
I would have weighed under 100 pounds
I would have been fed secretly by a compassionate combatant
I would not have known my buddy was executed with bamboo spears
I would have been 19 years old
I would have been from New Jersey
I would have clung to a silk scarf from my sweetheart
The scarf would have been taken away
I would have been beheaded at 4 p.m. on March 2, 1945
My abdomen would have been cut open
My liver would have been removed
It would have been prepared and eaten at an officer's sake party

My parents would get a letter stating *missing in action*

Bissonnett Boulevard Dogs

Winston Derden

In the time it took
to complete the loop
on the southern end of my walk,
a dog lay dead on Bissonnet.

A gray flannel terrier,
a working dog,
hit in extended stride,
a cone of blood

sprayed from his head
like a coup de grace,
he lay inconveniently
in the inbound lane.

Mocha-toking commuters
crawl past the corpse,
zombie-eyed riders
in the shotgun seat.

Their thoughts converge,
though their eyes never meet,
working dogs on the way to work
navigating a dangerous street.

The Horde's Prayer

Winston Derden

Our phantom who art imagined,
how hollow be thy name?

Thy kingdom's run,
thy will is done
on earth by those
who pretend guidance from heaven.

Give us this day our daily meds
and forgive us our trespasses
as we avenge those who trespass against us.

Leave us to seek out temptation,
but deliver us from consequence of evil.

For thy name is the key to power and self-glorification
for ever and ever.

Mother's Eyes

Nicholas Bailey

Tender affections,
Swift and slow movements,
The gasps and moans of pleasure
Like the winds through a field
Some screams and some cries
All leading to an amazing end
A seed, or rather many seeds, and her egg,
The soil of life
Not every seed grows,
But one is lucky
One is strong enough
Planted deep within
Provided with what it needs
Over time it grows, sprouting a new life, a new being,
Like a sprout from a seed
One day we are born,
Emerging from the soil
Showing the mothers hard work and devotion
Like a small thin stem,
We start out weak,
Our roots loosely planted on earth
Yet held tight in the mothers embrace
Cries and screams, silenced with gentle touches,
For we are fragile
More time passes,
We grow taller
Our limbs growing thicker
Slowly gaining strength
We start to stand on our own
But we start to differ now
The plant returns her devotion,
Reaching deeper for the mothers embrace
While we pull away
Shortening out roots
Lifting away

Craving freedom
Wanting to see the world
We pull away from mother
Resisting her pleading pull
And more time passes
We are standing on our own
While the sapling has grown sturdy
Stronger yet still relying in her
We age more and more,
Slowly realizing we envy the plant
Seeking to once again plant our roots
We finally settle down
Finding a partner in the crowds
We lower our roots again
Breaking through the ground
We look to the tree
Tall and sturdy, standing alone an proud
Yet always beside her
We lie in our bed with our partner,
Firmly planting our roots
Happy and finally satisfied
Looking in each others' eyes
Showing tender affections
Bodies joined as one
Swift and slow movements,
Moans and gasps escaping and another seed is planted
With the same old tree watching over, looking through her eyes
The eyes of mother

Origin

Linda Bratcher Wlodyka

together they
          swim,
                    together they
                              crawl,
                                        together they
                                                  walk.

they dance
          close together.

as if connected by a
tether,
          their togetherness
               in the wilderness
                    defies their
                              otherworldliness.

their harmonic oneness
                    entirely monogamistic,
                         spiritual yet physical,
                              a survival of the fittest,
                                        defies the critics.

even Darwin is optimistic.

Dance Underwater

Birdman 313

I can dance under water without getting
wet,
Swim the deepest sea to stay dry that's a
bet.
To walk under water to visit a peaceful
place,
I can dance under water and see your
face.
It's not magic or a sexual under water
dream,
The faith I have under water to flow up
stream.
I can dance under water without getting
wet,
Jump into the deep blue sea to hear the musical
set.
I can dance under water without any
fear,
Then relax under the moonlight without changing
gears.

Your Last Friend

Birdman 313

You are my last friend,
Even during the thunder that the Angels send.
Never hearing what I say,
Even though you see me every day.
It's fine what little hair you have parted,
But still denying you just farted.
We know the same old stories,
No matter who steals the glory?
Then tell hilarious lies,
All are friend's laugh who is up in the sky.
We are friends on a park bench,
Sipping on a drink and a hand roll smoke like Mr. Grinch.
Feeding the park yard birds,
Oooops one just dropped a turd.
Watching the pretty girls stroll with their dogs,
Wishing for younger days when you could jog.
Then the months come when it snows and rains,
The bench is frozen with an icy stain.
Then the months past to blossoms with the birds in spring,
Bring us back to our bench to hear the crickets sing.
Not feeling any older but glad to meet once more,
To see who has a new story to enjoy.
You no doubt is my best friend,
Years has past still no money to lend.
Share this cardboard to cover your feet,
Your shoes are worn from the miles you keep.
Beggars, vagrants and lonely hearts stop by,
Wanting to sit down to share a warm cry.
It has been a week since you were here,
Now my heart seeks loneliness to shed a tear.
But I won't give up your seat,
Knowing it is still warm from your body heat.
Now the raindrops become heavy from your absence,
Our cardboard seat cover what's left of your presence?
You are laughing at me saying I don't have enough since to come
      out of the rain,

Your only best friend in the world still has a heart full of pain.
Well you're not here for are daily chat,
I know you're coming so no need to spat.
Raining or not today you will appear,
Our time on the bench is growing apart it's the end of the year.
I know where you are,
You save me a seat up amongst heaven and stars.
You tell them about me,
I'm your best friend they will see.

Victory!

Chuck Taylor

I feel I'm hacking my way through heavy underbrush without my machete, trying to write this prose poem. I'm covered with sweat and all I want to do is lie down and sleep, but I know the fire ants will find me and bite me all over. I keep listening for the sound of a river, or the sound of a car, as I write this prose poem. Some sign of civilization, like a wire overhead. Soon it will be dark and I've barely begun. So many things I want to tell you, so many things we share in life, but life keeps getting in the way. I think it was Virginia Woolf who wrote of a painter who struggled at the easel for years trying to get her oil picture right, and she did, shortly before she died, and now the painting lies rolled up under the bed of a relative.

I've had ear infections, and before that I had my kidney removed for cancer. My daughter dropped out of college. The government is partially shut down and maybe soon I won't get a social security check. How will I buy food? How will I pay the runt? You need this prose poem, don't you? It is something you hunger for, almost like food. I plan to tell you that soon you will fall in love. Your soul mate is not far away and is searching for you as much as you are searching for him. I wish to tell you that there will be hard times, yes, but you will be mostly happy in life and you will be a success. That's my job. I'm the prose poet. The landlord has said he'll give me a month of rent free if I paint the outside of this duplex. He will buy the paint.

You see, miracles come along every day. Relief on the rent will give me a chance for some days off from working for Kelly Girl, and I can finish this prose poem, made especially for you. Look into the eyes of the poem now, please. Inside these letters I am looking back at you, and I want you to know that you are special. God made you for a purpose in his expanding universe with billions of galaxies. You may feel lonely at times, but I am here, your prose poem. I got through things. If I can do it, then you can do it. I have to end now, but please, carry on. Victory!

I pour a shot of whisky
(for Barry)
Chicory Poetry

I pour a shot of whisky
 it tastes like your
sweet & salty skin
as you lay with me
in the darkness

The Prose Poem and Einstein

Chuck Taylor

A former student of Einstein once told the prose poem that Einstein often carried a baseball bat. After that, the prose poem would be driving late at night, and suddenly Einstein would be in the car sitting next to him holding a bat.

"No, I never played baseball," said Einstein. "Baseball has never enjoyed a great popularity in Europe, but there was a small sports equipment store on my walk to work at the Patent Office, and I went in and bought one once.

I had no intention of threatening my fellow employees at the office. I merely like the heft of the bat now and then and think about the nature of time. At that point in my thinking, I believed that time was controlled somehow by the motion of electrons around atoms. I had this notion that if I swung the bat around my office I could knock plenty of electrons off their atoms and disrupt the flow of time.

During the lunch break, when everyone went out, I often set cheap clocks along the edge of my desk and smashed them one at a time with the baseball bats. You see, prose poem, I hated those clocks and their slow motion forward toward everyone's death. We were trapped by the clock's absolute notion of time and no one could escape it.

I wanted to escape death, so I had to come up with some other notion of time, and I did that. No doubt you've read my book on relativity, but I did not devise a definition of time that actually gave us any freedom. That's the trouble with science. It often inexorably leads you to conclusions that you don't want. We are not only in the noose of time, but we are surrounded and squeezed by space-time, which is actually one thing.

Our only hope is to get out of the universe, perhaps through a passageway deep in a dark hole, into an entirely different universe that works by different laws of physics.

That's why I always chose to make my appearance and ride with you, prose poem. Mathematics has reached its end. It has become obsessed with trivialities.

I am counting on your flights of fancy to lead us toward an answer.

Prose Poem Speaks
Chuck Taylor

In this prose poem the winds are no longer blue soft moans or sad hard wailing. The winds make a hardy mischievous laughter blowing down trees and houses.

In this prose poem the earth remains no longer passive, so full of graves silent as abandoned homes. It screams back when you stick a sharp shovel in its skin. Why are you surfacing me with all this asphalt and cement? I can hardly breathe anymore. I'm starting to suffocate. I need to slide down mountains to get myself free.

In this prose poem the stoic rocks are growing angry. They are leaving behind their silence. You humans, they say, you think you are so great, that you can crush us and push us around. Do you really think we will stay unmoved forever?

In this prose poem the rivers and seas are flexing their muscles. Humans have poured into their bodies so much poison they've had to swallow and swallow, yet the waters still slide with light flashes and sing with soft ripples. Yet they grow stronger and larger and need more land. They have just begun to sweep away shores and barriers, like a bear at Yellowstone ripping off the door on a car.

Dangerous Love (excerpts)

Nina Nicole

Chapter One

Lynx had his target right where he wanted him, that poor bastard had no idea that he was about to become someone's meal tonight, stepping across the street of downtown Atlanta Georgia, he was wearing his hit man gear, tight black muscle shirt, black jeans black tennis shoes the only thing he had on that wasn't the absence of color is his brown leather jacket this he wore with just about everything because even a cold blooded murderer had to keep some style...

...The kind of work that he did for a living was not approved among his kind but fuck if he needed the money he didn't have the luxury of being Mr. pretty boy with loads of cash in his bank account to piss away, born to a mother that was a prostitute in the year 1750 he was considered trash the moment he took his first breath of life back in those times people like him and his mother keep their mouths shut and their heads low you made due with what you had while staying happy about it; he learned as he got older to stay out of peoples way it wasn't easy bearing the whispers of everyone saying "there's the son of a whore" or the bastard that didn't know who his father was; he got used to it though.

He helped his mother out as much as he could by making water buckets out of wood then selling them in the next town, it was shit money but at least the woman that birthed him didn't have to sell her soul every night. When he turned twenty he kissed his mother goodbye on her tired aged stricken cheek and left all of the keep your eyes to the ground way of life behind then made his way to the nearest ship to America saving money wasn't easy but he had enough dough for a boat ride, London would never again be his home...

...Lynx knew this because he had spent a few nights coming to Passion; the best way to kill your prey is to know the exact time to strike...To his undead, hypersensitive ears it made him want to jam a swizzle stick through his ear and into his brain; the back door started to make a creaking sound, which meant that someone was about to come out of it. Lynx discarded his cigarette and stood up slowly stretching his bent knees that had been straining for a half hour, the person coming out of the club was his guy; right on time.

...Damn this guy smelled of marijuana and other various narcotics his blood was going to be the equivalent of a shit sandwich...Before his prey had a chance to respond Lynx had his fangs deep inside the man's neck as he felt the plasma enter his mouth he let the putrid sludge slip down his throat, with every deep pull he made, the man pushed and grabbed at him making gasping noises...He took a minute letting his canines retract back into his gums; wiping a rivulet of blood from his chin he looked at the guys puss he had the look of sheer terror as his mouth laid slack and his eyes all but popping out of his head.

...Riding on the high that shit sandwich gave to him Lynx made his way through the thinning crowd of club Passion strolling up to the bar and planting his ass on one of the stools flagging the bartender down "scotch", he hated that he could absorb and feel whatever that was in someone's blood stream definitely one of the downfalls of being undead he didn't know exactly what drug shit sandwich took but it made him feel like he was riding a tornado of highs and lows, antsy one minute, calm as a cucumber the next and he couldn't wait to get off the fucking ride. Not really needing the scotch that he called for he downed it anyway in one swallow letting the liquid burn in the back of his throat as well as for the taste of the bad blood, he was in here for one thing and one thing only, pussy.

Chapter Two

...She couldn't believe she was going to have to deal with this all over again; it had been six months since she had heard from him and she thought that he had found something else to do with his time, that he would finally leave her alone now looking at the message in front of her she knew that that was not going to happen Hey doll face did you miss me? She saved the number into her phone so that she would have warning of who it was next time he contacted her and he would be contacting her again she also had a feeling that this time it wasn't going to end so well that this time her life might be in danger...

...feeling as though she was all out of options she turned to face herself in the full length mirror she had hanging on the back of her room door. She stood there looking at the person she would have to become, she would have to become a survivor, her own protector; she dreaded the decision she was about to make but felt it was her only line of defense.

This Light
Dustin Pickering

Now the world falls silent
in reproach to the goddess of alms.
Her sand dollar face
completely worn by an escalade of days.

The laughter of white silence
and their promises, o the days.
Let the weeping come.

These ministers of freedom
are rebirths in complex rhythm.
We leave our stains on the world.

Let the silence engulf these rivers
broad, entrenched with gay surrender.

Unaware
Dustin Pickering

I remember envy.
His face like an angel
and a mouth strummed like a chord.
O blind eternity!

Within me there are glorious fires.
My mind, an elegant refuge.
At times I am unhappy,
but I lose my senses in the dark.

How Far

Dustin Pickering

Like breezes sweeping the
  golden apex of a mountain,
I will launch my beauty at the dawn hour.

Emptiness, o Word from breath,
  renounce the slender whisper!
The Word is first and must be made
  anew.
The Word is last will forever last.

We must make the night come closer.
With love, we will bend guiding eyes.
O how enlivening is this!
Shadow, your blood shall flow!

        but I cannot see the plan
        but I cannot reason from it
          other intuitions
        o See, see how far is the candle!

Incarnate Choice
Dustin Pickering

Incarnate choice
of broken solstices,
let lingering light lambaste
  against a hurried promise!

How are these motions still,
  and where are my lips?
Do I speak of vanity?

        o Poetry of straight midnight,
        your torso is hanging
          like a star
          in deepest sky.

Laurel leaves are the crown of dawn.
Are we in the famous room?
Is it a room of our own?

An Early Poem Concerning Catholicism
Dustin Pickering

Vague colors in nothingness, and sweet-scented Being:
do we see it?
Unity as discreet as sin–
  what does it contain?
My life, lived for you–
  to what purpose?
My heart is a shroud of glass.
When you ask of me its stained pieces shatter,
  piercing those questions burning in my soul.
Oh Carthage,
    why?
If it wasn't for her, who would you be?
Malls and fashions crack like a chalice on the concrete.
Deifying questions as the philosophies of my youth are lost...
O Carthage–
    why burn *now*?

Synapses

Leisl Weaver Miller

If I could unravel your whispers they would string across all eternity, never to meet their intentions, they would burn trying to follow me. If I could unfasten your kisses from my lips, they would float and hover and grip my astral geometry whilst they try to land squarely upon the center of love's symmetry. If I could unknot your navy blue gaze from the endless nights that tether me to this poetry I would dare not do it for I crave the way you flow into me. If I could unhitch the moments, the memories, the mystic movement and synergy from my shining mind, I think I would be better not to, for this is where you dwell and I know anytime I want to, I can find you. If I could unbutton your dancing swirling spirit from the door of my soul, I know that I would regret letting your spicy sweet essence go. If I could unwrap the dawning of the Aegean Sea, resuscitate tender death within me, feed the twirling butterflies that sit atop volcano's guarantee, I surely would, just so, you could be beside me. If I could untie our supple energy from one another, or even conceal it from my own heart, I know that I would not recover since this is the place where I's and If's disembarked. If I could unlock reality and guide it towards punctual eventuality, knowing what I know now, I certainly could rest happily in the cradled nest of ineffable love and the fresh blush of morn. If I could unhook the daring divides and shorten the synapses between our glances, instead of wishing you were here, or I, there, indeed I would fasten myself to the past, skip over the broken footsteps and fly away home to you.

Paper Doll

Leisl Weaver Miller

Arms and legs outstretched,
pinned by all appendages to the cork board blue sky.
She is a paper doll with saffron locks and a fluffy flowered violet dress.
Her turned out feet and little toes are bound, only by the aching flesh that knows
nakedness.
Her seraphic dreams are wired to the waving moonbeams and the dainty dew,
and of course, all the sweet by and by "I love you's".
Her apple eyes do wander as he flies by, so close, so, so very close,
almost touching fingertips, perhaps tinkering and fiddling with her pulsing
aubergine aura.
Then he darts away from her paper white lips! (No one has bothered to color
them in.)
She imagines that he must be taking a trip around the Sun
or a joyous voyage to Arcturus, or perhaps he is planning to meddle and mingle
amongst
the eternal pieces of morphemic clouds . . . waiting for the wet tingle,
trying to iron out the invisible wrinkles or maybe drumming up hollow symbols,
or possibly showering the people with false principles. . .

In the trenches of this black and gold galaxy, she becomes saturated with the
fantasy
that he will lift her to his thoughts and she will absorb his love instantly.
It's a snowflake's day, an icicles' climb, a stony halt kiss on the inner thigh.
It's a travesty, a comedy, a musical solution to languorous longevity.
It's a book that was never started, a chapter without an end,
a period with a question mark, a syllepsis without a friend.

Fastened in a forgotten corner, the vaulted firmament seems so much smaller
than a speck of stardust that can be traced to far away wonders, or astronomies
full of blunders!

There isn't any choice or compromise to stretch between secret anomalies,
only fierce regrets that cleave to canyons of dark distress. A sky wire anchored
and knitted between rows of strata create illusions of dancing mantras,
color bursting panoramas, and abracadabra pajamas.
Walking the wire, walking, walking, walking
until the rabbit runs, walking without talking, walking and chewing gum,
walking circles around the fire, walking on eggshells or glass,
sleep walking through rapid river waters, clutching river daughters,

grasping the reins of the cream colored ponies that drive solitude through valleys.
To heal the battered feet, to break away from ancient pinned up sleep,
to step, to leap, to fall into each other's arms at the end of it all,
knowing that faith was the real feat of it all. All along, pausing in hunger,
folding tabs tightly, skillfully trading inky lightning
for the pulpy pale thunder of far away soldiers. Writing letters
that resembles love and war, heaving throaty whispers on horizontal doors.
Being loved once, thrown away twice, covered three times before
paper clothes hit the cluttered milky floor. Chasing straight rainbows
out past the meadows. The revolving green gateways carry commotion,
deliver dead devotion, and a plethora of heart trending emotion.

Laying in weighted waters the chamber bed of her heart stutters,
the broken banging of whisper's echoes, the digging up of collagen fiber and
calcium phosphate,
blood and guts, a teddy bear stuffed of trust.
Flesh in the flesh, flesh on the flesh, flesh of my flesh!
Thorny oily scaffolding frames the fist of feelings constructed of innumerable
micro-bits of Photographs and Memories that never did exist.
Compartments emptied of invisible kisses and ember's embraces
leave the attics of her life walled up,
brick by brick by bloody boney brick—
a thirsty hidden crypt written in hieroglyphic arithmetic.
The center of the whole will never be known.
He holds onto delays, sheering moments from minute minutes,
showing favor to arranged seconds, owning nothing of his own!
Dotted line messages cut holes in her S. O. S. and
his bravery to love, or to be loved skips over leaving ships
throwing itself off of craggy angry creeping cliffs!
This love was always a suicide letter!
No end in sight, no mending fences,
only one hard beautiful truth concerning the damages—

All that needed to be done
was for someone to shade her parchment paper crisp lips
and give her a colorful kiss.

Zero has won.

Caretaker Mingles

Chad Sorg

Caretaker mingles
"I never wanted to own this land."
He mingles in the free air
there's no fence in sight
abstract exchanges are between men
Nature's work is non-contractual
Whose deed covers this land,
the toil, the blood that flowed,
whose hierarchy will blanket here
roughshod the paper
whose silent high basin layered, lawyered
The crow flies alone this afternoon looking down upon
The caretaker mingling

Human Pains and Growing Stains

John Davidson

Beating my skull against a nuclear bomb
wishing something would happen, but it never comes to pass.
Held together with lies and bloody surmise,
turning so ugly and crass.

Hell's own fury was but a glimmer, to catch the fly in its trap.
Ripping at wings and feeble things, to watch blood run like sap.

Feverish lines scratched on the walls from an oracle of bleeding nails.
Never to reach from bones and bleach, to decipher these runes and
tales.

I tried to say congratulations, but it came out like doom.
Beating my skull against a nuclear bomb, wishing something would
finally....
BOOM!

Judas by Proximity

John Davidson

Wig-onometry split and injected with lies, morose decisions in the
anatomy of flies.

A hushed argument I lost to myself, amid the clamoring roar.
A private joke I told to myself, sprawled next to you on the floor.

Judas by proximity, traitor by inches and feet.
Marred by another hypocritical mother, strangled in the sheets.

French doors creep open in my mind, to release this whimsical error.
The burden shifted on my back, contorting the load and bearer.

Shamelessly addicted to a thing called treason, that threatens this fragile
state.
And rolling eyes purge good byes, from the ashes on my plate.

Judas by proximity, liar by shades and degrees.
Made a mud angel in heaven's basement, where all watch but no one
sees.

The Book Of Life

Chicory Poetry

The book of life
Is merely
An inventory
Of the bridges
That cross back
(& over)
In time

Bridges & books
Both can be burned
By the dim light
Of smoke & embers
Of the broken dawn
Realization

We are lost

My Country, Too

Marcie Eanes

My voice rises from the souls of many generations
Proud men and women pulse through my veins;
Their voices choked silent
    while enduring unspeakable horrors
On ships,
    plantations,
    segregation
All begging entitled few to hear words
"I AM American" without judgments

I take my place in the struggle,
Grabbing life with both hands,
  understanding sacrifices of those before.
Every sunrise is another chance to do best!
There is common ground in all people's stories
  who inhabit these shores
When ears listen fully and brain rejects ideas
Planted solely for division

No one race fought more for freedoms
Wars call all
  to sacrifice under Old Glory's colors
Our country needs united to finally move forward
It takes an entire village, alive with booming voices
To take to heart all the promises
    in those words spoken
When saying
  "I pledge...."

Texas Vision Center
Richard Peake

The sign blazes forth in the shopping mall.
Guy sees it. He starts contemplating
visions. Those that have them become
visionaries–Visionary! How wonderful–
marked by foresight, having dreams, revelations,
a seer whose mystical acts of seeing
conjure the supernatural–sight, discernment–
creating a better view of reality–altering
our defective world. Guy decides to start a vision center
of his own, a place for new ideas, far out from city
noise and smog, where air is clearer and he can
build in Hill Country soaring high enough to allow sights
of Gulf waters and out westward beyond hill country
to imagination's limits. He'll fit people's glasses
so that they'll see through shibboleths destroying
ability to dream–wide open spaces of Texas
will create possibilities for seeing human achievements,
matching prairie winds with minds expansive
as Texas' horizons. He'll fit glasses to cut through smog,
unkindness, sloth, and bigotry. His clients will reach
new dimensions. They'll see that being biggest
is not always best, that quality, not quantity
gives lasting visions, that executing innocents
to avoid seeing guilty go free leads to horrid nightmares,
not truth. They'll find prairie more beautiful
than pock-marked pavement and housing
and think sunsets beat video games for producing peace
and fulfillment. They'll see that their energy
problems come from within, not without–they'll learn
to travel to new worlds without rocketing into space.
They'll dream a better universe, learn
ordinary people can be visionaries.

Occupation

Jenuine Poetess

has it really been two years
two years
since the occupation
of
a moment
a place
in all of time
and space
a dream
a vision
a movement

since the occupation of a
rEVOLution?

but it wasn't just then...

yes
I am remembering now
it began earlier
long before
spanning an entire lifetime

for years
the changes
were ever so slight
the merest of flickers
there were moments
flashes of recognition
yet not the freedom
to fully become

and then there came a time
for discovering
for moving in

I was tentative
untrusting of myself
new
in my own skin
my own thoughts
my own understanding
learning how to take up space
all of the space
within myself
no longer
timid in the
quiet corners of my being
I
cleared cobwebs from
my throat
learning to recognize
to listen for
the sound of my own voice

at first I faltered
when others
questioned
doubted or
laughingly mocked this me
new and ancient
all at once
a clumsy paradox
of deconstructed renovations

the occupation of myself
was never hostile
no violent take over
it was a willing letting in of
consciousness
a throwing open of curtains
in a too-long dark room
uncomfortable at first
shocking

Waterplay at the Base of Luther's Canyon
(*outside Huntsville, Texas*)

David Cowen

amidst the low trees of the hollow
of Luther's Creek,
in clear water
running shallow over red iron,
hidden deep from the farmer's ire,
I playfully splashed your white blouse
and saw the red buds of your nipples
begin to form against the two pockets,
still buttoned;
I stopped for a moment in our gambol
of dampness
eyes fixated on your skin exposing

your face
reddening as you realized
the blood in my cheeks
was from more than folly
turned into the sun
taking your innocence from me
to hide
in the chasteness of dryness.

BOOK REVIEWS

"I Took My Barrio on a Road Trip" by Edward Vidaurre
PW Covington

Edward Vidaurre is one the driving forces behind the explosion in literature and art coming out of Texas' Rio Grande Valley region in these days. This collection, published by Slough Press, offers a very personal and dynamic glimpse into the journey that brought both Edward's poetry and his person to this point.

"I Took My Barrio on a Road Trip" is a tale of soul always searching; it is a story of a man that has found a home. It is a tale of a culture that exists anywhere you take your heart and your history. His poetry tells us about the past, and it looks to the future, all while seeking to define itself in the ever-ending present.

I am not Chicano, but I have found a brother's voice in the pieces "Summer in El Salvador" and "The Bullet of '91". I did not grow up in the housing projects of Los Angeles, yet I, also, am vested in the story of "Her Name was Maria".

These poems each stand on their own merit and under their own power, but when taken together, this book becomes something greater than the sum of its parts. Divided into three, roughly chronological sections, exploring this collection leaves the reader with the feeling of having gotten to know a new friend, someone that CAN understand, because he HAS lived. Edward Vidaurre invites us all along as fellow travelers, knowing very well that we all are here to share the best and the worst life has to give us.

Buy this book of poetry, and if your travels every bring you to deep South Texas, do what you can to see Edward Vidaurre read, I promise, you will find a friend.

"I Took My Barrio on a Road Trip" is available through Amazon, B&N, and directly from Slough Press www.sloughpressbooks.com.

"Earth and Stars: Poems 2007-2010" by Richard Peake
Dustin Pickering

I cannot briefly glance through the poems of *Earth and Stars* because I am also advised to read them aloud by the author, Richard H. Peake. Should I want to spend only a moment trekking the wild of Peake's poems? Wouldn't I then miss the intricacy of language and style, and also blind my eye to the intimate truth? *Earth and Stars* is densely populated with strange creatures and moments. In participating through my readership, I am the voyeur of a natural world created with "transportation of thought" ("Electric Wings for *Ars Poetica*").

The common reader will visit life anew to learn bravery, contemplation and playfulness. Moments we seize through these pages offer wisdom and adventure. The reader examines death and resolution, effort and joy. Peake's vision will astound the reader with deep intelligence and common-sense penetration of subject matter. His long poem "War Games" recounts his World War II childhood. There are other poems that contain national and personal history. Peake is saddened by the gutting of our manned flight space program, but his disappointment is due to the loss of potential rather than contempt for the order of things. "The Pollination Game's Gone Bad" doesn't even hint at this same theme. Instead, it informs us of parasites and queen bees that trouble other bees. Upon deeper thinking, we may read into the poems an expression of similarities between human society and the natural order. In spite of losses, much is gained from having a perceptive eye.

The collection winds to a close with poems reflecting on nature's intimate artistic life. "The Southland's Jazzbird" contains witty remarks about human musicians who envy birdsong. The most unsavory mockingbird trills will only be heard in the North where no competition exists to put them to shame.

As one of Peake's many publishers, I must admit I envy his breadth of knowledge and study. His tributes are touching and his insights inspire deep thought and appreciation. I know his words are sincere, and that much guided effort is placed in the structure of this book. It will not only entertain and inspire the reader with its many musings, but will also stir feelings of trust in Providence. I feel invited into a new world and wilderness.

Not Quite A Political Column

As time goes on it gets more and more difficult to remain outside of the conjured left-right political paradigm. What's most upsetting often is the lack of representation for the pro-humanist. One good example is the current healthcare fiasco farce. Human suffering is not a commodity. Disease is not a means to sustain a profit or create a market but a problem to be solved. Medicare and medicaid are good but incomplete. The current madness found in "Obamacare" does little to eliminate the problem other than line the pockets of the insurance industry, as it was intended.

The person most directly responsible for the 87-page "white" paper that served as the blueprint for what would eventually become Obamacare is Liz Fowler. Before she worked for the Obama administration she was the Vice President of Public Policy and External affairs for Wellpoint, a large managed healthcare company under the Blue Cross and Blue Shield Association.

What this amounts to is that the current healthcare legislation was primarily written by a public relations officer for the "managed" healthcare industry. Obamacare's primary intention is to force everyone into the unnecessary and parasitic scam known as insurance. It shouldn't come as a surprise to anyone that the ludicrous launch of Obamacare was as sloppy and pointless as the very notion of anything other than a single payer health system.

The United States has one of the worst infant mortality rates and life expectancy rates in the developed world. Coupled with the obesity epidemic and the rise in diabetes, it doesn't take a brain surgeon to notice the health crisis in our society. It all points to a failed system that feeds the vultures at the top while leaving everyone else to suffer. The United States is also the only major developed nation that doesn't have a universal non-profit health insurance option. As a taxpayer I'm already paying taxes for those that qualify for medicare and medicaid, but am unable to receive the benefits of these limited but effective programs. It seems to me that expanding medicare to include all citizens instead of bailing out and nurturing the health insurance industry is the proper road to a real solution.

My argument couldn't be simpler. All I ask is that we, as a country, take all the money, effort, and time to build bombs and bullets and merely redirect it towards taking care of our elderly, educating our young, and providing a means to better the standard of living for all working class/age people. Bombs or books, it's that simple.

26061328R00033

Made in the USA
Charleston, SC
23 January 2014